The Walt McDonald First-Book Series in Poetry

Robert A. Fink, *editor*

SERVICE

SERVICE

poems

BRUCE LACK

introduction by Robert A. Fink

Texas Tech University Press

This book is typeset in Adobe Garamond. The paper used in this book meets
the minimum requirements of ANSI/NISO Z39.48-1992 (R1997). ∞

Designed by Ryan Miller

Library of Congress Cataloging-in-Publication Data
Lack, Bruce.
        [Poems. Selections]
    Service : poems / Bruce Lack ; introduction by Robert A Fink.
        pages cm. — (Walt McDonald first-book series)
        ISBN 978-0-89672-919-3 (hardback) — ISBN 978-0-89672-920-
9 (paperback) — ISBN 978-0-89672-921-6 (e-book)
    I. Title.
    PS3611.A347A6 2015
    811'.6—dc23

    2014044596

15 16 17 18 19 20 21 22 23 / 9 8 7 6 5 4 3 2 1

Texas Tech University Press
Box 41037
Lubbock, Texas 79409-1037 USA
800.832.4042
ttup@ttu.edu
www.ttupress.org

For my wife, Liz, my father, and the U.S. Marines:
each their respective World's Finest.

CONTENTS

III.

INTRODUCTION

"I WILL SHOW YOU FEAR IN A HANDFUL OF DUST."

    T. S. Eliot—"The Waste Land"

"BRING ME TO THE BRINK OF MOUNTAINS, MYSTIC
DREAD, RAPTURE OF FEAR I FEEL AND . . . FAIL.
STILL: THE SWALLOW SLICING BLUE IS BEAUTIFUL.
STILL: THE CLOUD-TUGGED BELL TOWER'S FROZEN MUSIC."

    Christian Wiman—Translation of the opening stanza from
    Osip Mandelstam's "Bring Me To The Brink."

Reading Bruce Lack's *Service*, we discover ourselves *engaged*, learning, and remembering the rules of engagement ("Rules of Engagement Pop-Quiz"). Before we know it, we are no longer the *new guy* ("FNG"), the one who, deployed, counts the days; who, keeping a calendar, drives himself crazy; the one who doesn't know any better ("The War According To Master Sergeant Marsh"). We are "here for the duration" ("The War According to Master Sergeant Marsh"). We will talk to God. We will beg Jesus to "look away" ("Thirteen Months of Talking to God"), but *we* will not be able to.

Service was written for us, written to us. This is our Let Me Tell You . . . book. The title of Miller Williams' poem "Let Me Tell You" also functions as the poem's opening line, followed by "how to do it from the beginning. / First notice everything." Williams is instructing students in the art of writing poems. Bruce Lack, his Drill Instructor, Master Sergeant Marsh, and numerous other voices of combat veteran Marines instruct us in the craft of staying alive, specifically in Fallujah, Iraq. "First notice everything": scan the road, the roadside, for anything that looks innocent—that "jumble of children's toys," the "Coke can," a "mangled soccer ball, / folding chair, battered road sign, window frame" ("Scanning"). "That body is a bomb. They put a bomb in a corpse" ("That Feeling You Can Only Describe in Arabic"). Innocence will kill you.

"Not me," you're thinking, and I agree. You and I are not reading *Service* as a survival manual. We're too young, too old, too comfortable, too removed to be called to service in a Waste Land where in order to survive and come back home to our mothers who "can't read / our expressions any longer," we must pay the price of "becoming strangers to everyone / but each other," other Marines the only ones who "can see each other's faces" ("Our War," No. 5). We have not earned their new name, the right to call ourselves "*Marine . . .* , noble yet martial," the final syllable a scream ("Our War," No. 1. "How To Get A Man To Kill Another Man").

We comfort ourselves with assurances—the "war is going well" ("Our War," No. 10), offering our "adulation," thanks for their "*service*" ("Our War," No. 12)—"young old men" who "haven't legally bought a beer, / and yet they've seen friends die, / known survivor's rage" ("Our War," No. 14). These young, old veterans understand we "mean no harm," only wanting "to know / what it was like without having to go" ("Our War," No. 13). Bruce Lack provides the answer, taking us to that place deep within, the place we did not know.

"I told the truth as well I could," the persona of "David Gomez: El Paso, Texas" says. This is what Bruce Lack is offering in *Service*, the Truth of his experience—complex, ambiguous, paradoxical, contradictory, impossible. Truth. The book's three sections transport us from innocence to experience to silence, rage, the "long, deep strobe of guilt" ("A Reminder I Don't Need") and pride, and finally to our unexpected destination—Love, a wife's steadfast patience, healing.

Section I contains fifteen poems that develop a "how to" approach to *service* in Iraq, how to prepare a Marine, how to anticipate doing his duty and getting back home, back to the *world* he won't recognize, the world that will no longer recognize him. "We were born too late to be good guys" ("How We Are Sick"). Fallujah is not the "Land where my fathers died! Land of the Pilgrims' pride!" It is "hardscrabble ground, / the ground that won't accept water / when it comes, that grows only spite," the "dirt / from which your enemies sprang" ("How Not To Write A War Poem"), a land where "that dead boy will be named a martyr / by the man building bombs too small to wear himself" ("How We Are Sick"). Here, Marines confront horrors as well as The Horror of Joseph Conrad's *Heart of Darkness*. So much to fear: "cordless phones, / video cameras, dead animals stuffed with jacks and Semtex, loose wires leading anywhere," the "flat stares" of Iraqis, "the folds of long robes" ("Last Day in Fallujah"). To survive, Marines have to "*protect each other / every minute*," keep the body awake—"*that stupid, animal engine— / that falls asleep*," keep walking, "*thankful for the pain / you can still feel*" ("A Teaching Moment"). And if the Marine preparing to leave Fallujah could be a *good guy*, might the Iraqis show him that he "could come back / here someday, beg and grant forgiveness, / embrace you bastards and be better for it, somehow" ("Last Day in Fallujah")?

Section II offers a fifteen-poem sonnet sequence defining the Marines' unique experience in this *their* war, not the newsreel Iwo Jima flag-raising war of their grandfathers and great-grandfathers, not the war of their fathers whose children now must be turned into killers scrambling "to find a way to bear this," discovering "there is no such way" ("Our War," No. 2). All will come to wear "the taut, terrible smiles" ("Our War," No. 6). *Our war* sounds like it "is going well," the "big guns" booming, artillery gunners "killing with trigonometry," a "rebuttal" to "incoming's treble," the sounds presaging "the kind of day you'll have tomorrow, / though it doesn't matter to anyone else" ("Our War," No. 10). Back home the war *is going well.* Back in *the world*, Marines will not be able to bear "the thanks for our *service*, / as if we knew what that word meant, before"; what they will bear is "the terrible gravity of coming back, / everything becoming heavy faster / than the speed of pain" ("Our War," No. 12), their lives no longer measured in length, but in depth, their eyes telling their story, their best desire—to "leave this desert clean, / a reminder to the world—live better" ("Our War," No. 14). All war is the same.

The fourteen poems of Section III depict the effects of *service* on veterans returning home, the consequences of this service. What Bruce Lack knows is that parents "don't get the same son back" ("David Gomez: El Paso, Texas"). Returning Marines don't know how to carry

xiv

themselves without the weight, both literal and symbolic, of combat, and it "terrifies" them that they "miss it" ("Get Some"). The persona of "Hadji" thought he would be "all right" returning home "on my feet," though he "can't / remember how to sleep / a night through" ("Hadji"). And, ironically, part of what the persona misses would be exchanging fire "with men no less strange than ourselves," in a city where despair is winning, and "these people—they never, ever look up, / just keep trying to stare themselves into the graces of a kinder god," what the Marines seem to be trying to do both in Fallujah and back home in the world ("In Heaven There Are No Doors").

The enemy understood, unlike the people back home "who couldn't begin to understand," ignorantly, innocently, "talking down to you" ("In Heaven There Are No Doors"), clapping you on the shoulder and smiling "as if at a secret only we two share, as if we / share anything at all" ("Small Talk"). The question becomes how does one go about "getting clean," getting the blood off your hands, the "half-moons of dull red / at the base of my fingernails" resistant to all cleansers ("Small Talk"). And your mother has "not been taught to see [you] / anymore" ("First Supper Back"). You would return to preserving life, even that of a bee—"A Marine Corps bee" tenaciously "butting against [your] kitchen window" ("A Reminder I Don't Need"). If you could. If it were possible. The persona of "Suicide Days" confesses that failing to rescue the bee, today he "could run / back to my recruiter, out to the desert / or the mountains."

Thank God he has a wife, his hope for a return to normalcy—hair ties left all over the house, spattering the sink's ledge, making rings on the coffee table, constricting furniture arms ("Without Regard"). Thank God she is there, looking up from her book, asking, "*What's the matter?*" ("Scanning"). Because of his wife, Bruce Lack will fashion a new mission statement. Today he will sit down and "write a poem that won't make my wife cry. / One that's not about war, or if it is, / about some uplifting facet," something "only a poet could notice" ("Mission Statement"), something Miller Williams had in mind, not what Master Sergeant Marsh cautioned against overlooking. As Osip Mandelstam still saw beauty in "the swallow slicing blue," the "cloud-tugged bell tower's frozen music," Bruce Lack maybe will find poetry in "a desert rose that survived where / my platoon mates did not," maybe in "the boy we didn't kill / because he put away his cell phone" ("Mission Statement"). This poem "will / be about some best version" of Bruce Lack, and when he reads it to his wife, they will smile *as if* she has not learned "the perfect technique" of gentling him, easing his nightmare breathing, not to wake him, but "always enough to / get me out" ("Mission Statement").

Bruce Lack has experienced us in war, the combat he and his fellow Marines experienced in Fallujah. We have learned what not to say, what not to ask, though he recognizes we want to know if he thinks we could "kill anyone," the *animal* in us rising to our fists, our trigger finger. Because we have survived *Service*, we don't need to ask. He has frightened and prided us into silence. Of course he would tell us, "but only in a whisper / so come closer, / where I can reach you" ("Small Talk"). And we did. And he did.

ACKNOWLEDGMENTS

My sincerest gratitude goes to the men and women of United States Marine Corps, 9th Communications Battalion, Alpha Company who served in Operation Iraqi Freedom II in all its permutations from 2003–2007. And of course, the entire community of my fellow veterans: I hope it's clear that this book is for you. Welcome home.

I would like to thank the Helen Zell Writers' Program at the University of Michigan—most notably and in no particular order: Laura Kasischke, Linda Gregerson, Lorna Goodison, and Keith Taylor. I would also like to especially thank Gala Mukomolova, Claire Skinner, Tina Richardson, and Airea Matthews for going above and beyond the call of duty in rendering support and critical advice in the completion of this book.

"Rules of Engagement Pop Quiz" owes an obvious debt, I think, to Nick Lantz's brilliant poem "Will There Be More Than One 'Questioner'?"

"In Heaven There Are No Doors" owes a similar, though less obvious, debt—beyond just the epigraph—to William Olsen's poem "This Heaven"

"FNG," "Hadji," and "Get Some" won Second Place in the Winning Writers' War Poetry Contest, 2010

"No Applicable Regulations" was an Honorable Mention in the Winning Writers' War Poetry Contest, 2011.

A version of "Our War" won the Theodore Roethke Prize in at the University of Michigan in 2012. It was also published in Michigan Quarterly Review.

An excerpt of this book won a Jule and Avery Hopwood Award for poetry at the University of Michigan in 2013.

"David Gomez: El Paso, Texas" appeared in the Rufous City Review.

SERVICE

I

FNG

This is your rack—keep it made and sleep on top of the covers. This is your dresser; this, your wall locker. Keep them locked. There's only one thief around here: everyone else is just trying to get their shit back. This is the shop. Be here tomorrow morning dressed to run. If you fall out of a run, God help you. This is how to cut your own hair. This is how to roll your sleeves. This is how to blouse your boots. This is how to wear your cover. This is how to salute. Always keep your right hand free in case you need to salute. These are your friends now. Memorize their names and home towns. This is town. This is where we eat when we go to town. This is where we drink when we go to town. They don't ask for ID, so don't worry. You buy the first round until we get a new guy. Never fight here. If you do fight here, don't get caught. If you get caught, call me first. I'll bail you out, but God help you. This is your weapon. Break it down shotgun style and check the bolt. Reassemble and do function check. If it's good, memorize the serial number. BZO it and memorize the BZO. When you go to the rifle range, shoot Expert. If you can't shoot Expert, shoot Sharpshooter for sure.

This is your fire-team. You're the smallest guy, so you're the rifleman. When you're on point, your eyes and sights are connected. If you look where your rifle isn't, God help you. If you see something, hear something, get a bad feeling about anything, say so. Any little thing could be the difference. This is how to lace your boots so we can cut them off if we need to. Label all your clothes in case we can't identify you any other way. This is your poncho. It's also a tent, a roof, a blanket, a pillow, a windbreak, a bag, a sail. Carry it everywhere. This is deployment. Don't write home too much. Don't think about home. When they shoot, make yourself small. Make sure you can identify an IED. This is how you breach a door. This is your sector of fire. Always assault *towards* an ambush. Don't freeze.

This is combat. Don't freak out. This is how you tie a tourniquet. This is how you treat a sucking chest wound. Breathing is more important than bleeding. Start the breathing, stop the bleeding, protect the wound, treat for shock. Nothing works in this fucking place. This is how you wrap a body in a poncho. It is also a shroud. Don't freak out.

This is home. Don't try to get it all back in one day. Give yourself time. Give your family time. Don't hurt anyone. Don't hurt yourself. Talk to us because we're the only ones who'll get it anyway. See you tomorrow.

How Not To Write A War Poem

Never go.
Never put boots to sand, never stand
beneath Allah's sun,
breathing the dust
of a city that hates you in every detail—

every animal vectoring disease,
wind always pounding
grit into your face, cementing the creases
at the corners of your eyes no matter
how you face away.

There's a metaphor
in the hardscrabble ground,
the ground that won't accept water
when it comes, that grows only spite,
that keeps breaking entrenching tools
until you just find a pickaxe and
go to war for real,

breaking the ground, breaking
the land, destroying the dirt
from which your enemies sprang
and wishing for salt to sow.
Never go.

The War According to Master Sergeant Marsh

Keep up, devil dog, we don't got much time—
I walk, I talk, you listen and soak
up this hip-pocket class, oorah?
Wear shoes in the shower if you don't want athlete's foot
or something third-world worse.
Breakfast is the most reliable meal out here,
and it's the same every day.
Don't give these people a thumbs up,
it means something different here.
Check email once a week, call home once a month
at the most—you're here for the duration,
so just be here.

You clean your rifle every goddamn day unless
you got something better to do than stay alive.

Shave your face, Marine. Deployment 'staches
are unsat and unsanitary. Don't kick that soccer ball.
You know what, if you didn't put it there,
don't pick up it—goes for anything
on the ground. These coward fucks
put Semtex in everything. Don't bother
learning Arabic. Alls you need to know
how to say is 'stop' and 'open the trunk.'

Don't count the days, keep a calendar, or even look at one:
guys who do that drive themselves crazy. I don't
even know what day it is.

Jesus Christ, get up
off the deck, hard-charger,
incoming happens all the time.
If you heard it, it didn't hit you.

How We Are Sick

A man imbeds ball-bearings in the soft
explosive putty molded to a boy's body
while turret gunners choose the mix of songs
they'll be listening to when they kill him.
If they don't break, we won't. This is how we are sick.

I preferred oldies—there was something soothing,
something transportive, about listening to
The Del Vikings, bobbing, dipping,
sweeping the barrel like a night of sock-hopping
with a USO girl so damned pretty
I couldn't get my mind around

her eyes seeing only my uniform,
and I'm fine if sex is off the table
because we can still push just shy.

That never happened, of course, but should have.

We were born too late to be good guys,
though families who don't know any better
and those hoping to get elected off our backs
will call us heroes, just the same
as that dead boy will be named a martyr
by the man building bombs too small to wear himself.

When Reid Died

He looks more
real than ever,
more real
than any of us
still walking,
like the most real
thing we'll ever see,
and he's still
so fucking
heavy.

Long as I'm Wishing

I want to not be talking to the chaplain, sir, no offense. But if God's involved, I want breakfast anytime and Motown in the chow hall. I want a supermodel—any one, it doesn't matter—in my trailer when I get back. I want sweat to stop running down the backs of my legs inside these bloused trousers. I want a ten minute shower and a beach towel. I want this shithole desert to bloom—farmers are too tired to terrorize anybody. If God is in it, I want time travel. I want to have checked the rooftop where that shot came from two seconds earlier. Anything to not have been standing there, not have gasped the mist of blood into my lungs when the round punched through his neck—did you know you could do that, sir, breathe blood?

A Teaching Moment

Davis presses his mattress over his head and marches
circles around his trailer all night long.
Through two gallons of water,
through his own vomit and tears
and shame, through the full-throated
whines he doesn't know he's making.

We protect each other
every minute, Davis,
every fucking one.

I know the way earplugs and liquid heat
make everything unreal, the way rumbling engine
and rising core body temperatures
make falling asleep in a Humvee,
even the lead vehicle, easy
as breathing.

You do it again and I will shoot you myself.

I can see you're sorry, Davis, in your mind
you're sorry, but it's your body—that stupid, animal engine—
that falls asleep. Keep walking, and be thankful for the pain
you can still feel.

I'll dance at your wedding Davis—
let's just get there.

That Feeling You Can Only Describe in Arabic

That body is a bomb. They put a bomb in a corpse. That dead person is going to explode because he's a bomb. He is a man, Improvised into an Explosive Device. That corpse is going to blow up. That body is a bomb. He is dead, and he is a bomb. That body right there, left to the sun and flies, fetched up pathetic and naked in a doorway, his arms outstretched as if with a simple hand up he'd just be on his way, is a bomb. They put a bomb in a dead man's body. That body is a bomb. We have to kill them twice now.

Lessons for the Assholes from Blackwater: All These Things Can Kill You

Sand flies, leishmaniasis,
overconfidence,
anthrax, smallpox—also the vaccinations
for anthrax
and smallpox—
scorpion venom, anaphylaxis,
overconfidence,
sepsis, burns, septic burns,
electrocution, dehydration,
friendly fire, enemy fire,
accidental discharge, intentional discharge,
land mines, claymore mines,
RPGs, IEDs,
getting ambushed, overconfidence,
Humvees overturning, overwhelming numbers,
getting hung upside down from a bridge.

The Last Five Minutes

All the blood I've ever bled
wouldn't come close
to what Maurice has lost
in the last five minutes.

It took three to find him
in the ruin a mortar makes
of office space, another
half-minute of triage:
Steelers jersey shredded
by whickering shards of circuit boards
and computing tower, glasses askew
but still on, black skin gone over grey,
charred paper scraps in his civilian goatee,
blown out of his shoes—his one shoe,
his right shoe. His left is gone.

Function now. Send your mind away
and tourniquet the leg that isn't, smash a bandage
hard on the thigh where a knee should be
and squeeze, breathe through your mouth,
keep the gag reflex down,
and talk, say Maurice
you're going home,
you're going on a Blackhawk and out,
you are not alone, you'll walk
again and be twenty pounds lighter
besides, keep your eyes open, man,
and you can come to Christmas
with my family if you just try to stay awake
for the next five minutes, hey,
I've got a sister who's single

and could do worse, come on, you're going
to Landstuhl for medical, there's a hot
German nurse and real food for you—

Fill the silence with yourself.
And when the corpsmen come
to take Maurice from you,
close his eyes,
and take the new bandage
and tourniquet to replace
the ones you lost.

Plea to Heaven

Furlong had a beautiful voice, Gabriel.
Archangel, take back that mortar.
Unwhistle it over the wall,
sound that long note in reverse,
and we will make for you such music—

> Then blow that trumpet
> motherfucker, if you've got something
> that'll impress us now.

Rules of Engagement Pop-Quiz

When you find the man you believe
is responsible for the mortars
will you bother with the interpreter?

Will you grab him by his robes
and shake him, screaming in English?

Will you wait to see if he understands you?
Will you wait to see if he understands you but pretends not to?

Will you tell him he isn't a person to you anymore?

Will you pull him close and breathe deep though he stinks?
Will you smell oil? Gasoline? Sterno? Will you want to?

Will you want it enough to imagine it?

Will he trip when you push him away?
Will you remember the Rules of Engagement?
Will you perceive an imminent threat to your life
or the lives of your fellow Marines?
Will you rack your weapon's charging handle?
Will you keep your finger straight and off the trigger,
or will you be ready to fire?
Will you keep your weapon on safe
or will you intend to fire?
Will you be pointing your weapon at something you do not
intend to shoot?
Or not?

When he pisses himself, will you let him walk away?

Thirteen Months of Talking to God

Lord help
me help us all
Christ Almighty Jesus
let him
stick his head
up
again oh
Jesus—
if you're there,
look away.

No Applicable Regulations

Scorpions find whatever shade they can, wait out the day
in the manner of cold-blooded things,
sheltered from heat that beats like a hammer.

We found them under sandbags. We forgot,
sometimes, our gloves. Stuck fingers in unguarded,
welcomed the sting, the fall, the one chance

we ever got to shirk duties and take ease.
The other wounded, their shrapnel-ruined flesh
that, if proven to be inflicted by the enemy,

earns them the right to wear Purple Hearts
alongside their scars. Friendly fire, accidents, and scorpions
get you nothing but wounded.

Now, snow melts on upside down boots—
the insides sodden, though there aren't,
and have never been, spiders here

known to take refuge in boots. Habits from the old life,
like Uncle Joe breaking filters off cigarettes,
playing fiddle on the back porch,

or betting a dollar on picking up tough spares.
Nothing is the same. Those ways give way.
Joe was in the ground two months before

the Chaplain pulled me from my gunner seat
to let me know that, since the man hadn't raised
me—was, after all, already dead and buried—

there being no applicable regulations,
I could not expect to be sent home over it.

Provoked, they posture up, all armor plating,
pugilistic claws held to faces. Ill-intent
dressed in slick black chitin,
they look like what they mean. Not like us,
saying "my condolences" by means of offering condolence,
praying only for our own.

Last Day in Fallujah

Take in the hung laundry
obscuring my sight lines,
sweep up your trash piles and burn
them, even, so long as I know
they won't blow up
and I'll start caring if this city still stands.

Cut the filament wires
stretched, humming for our throats,
across your roads, keep your
open hands in the open,
and keep peace with me
this one day.

You've shown me fear in cordless phones,
video cameras, dead animals stuffed with jacks and Semtex,
loose wires leading anywhere, your flat stares,
the folds of long robes, your raised voices,
startling glottal syllables—

you've shown what heavy caliber
7.62's do to folks who vote,
head-shot where they knelt,
and left for us to find.

Now show me that I could come back
here someday, beg and grant forgiveness,
embrace you bastards and be better for it, somehow.
Show me a smile without picturing me dead.
Show me an un-chipped cup of chai
sitting on a jersey barrier pocked
with bullet holes.

II

Our War

I. HOW TO GET A MAN TO KILL ANOTHER MAN

It's damned difficult.
Joe Blow off the street might—only
might—and only when panic's last
extremity takes his mind
from him and leaves the animal
thing behind: the thing that abandons
drowning strangers to the waves,
that kills anything but itself.
Much harder to convince the man to murder,
to backshoot someone who never knows he's there.
He has to be made something else first,
needs a new name to call himself.
Marine sounds right, noble yet martial,
teeth gritted around the last syllable: *Marine.*

2.

Teeth gritted around the last syllable: *Marine*
doesn't sound the same now someone's screaming
in your face from makeout distance
about how you would've made a perfect abortion
and you've never felt less like a killer—
a killer doesn't spend so much time scared shitless,
convinced a fatal error's been committed,
the miscarriage of his life.
The part that still thinks of itself by its name scratches
and scrambles to find a way to bear this:
there is no such way. The Name collapses
in on itself, curls fetal and relents
because there's animal underneath all the way to the bedrock.
It becomes easier to imagine killing.

3.

It becomes easier to imagine killing
as Drill Instructors show the ways and the animal eats it up,
keeps the body moving through the beatings
disguised as training, the grinding exhaustion and hunger—
the animal would crawl this body over burning coals
to learn another way to crush the cervical vertebrae:
the animal worries only that hands this small
may not be able to manage it.
The human body, though, is delicate—
X pounds of pressure shatters any bone you like.
It's as pleasing, in its way, as getting all of a fastball,
knowing by the vibrations in your palms
that it's gone, that bones never heal quite right, that
horrors come naturally to us all after a fashion.

4.

Horrors come naturally to us all, after a fashion—
put enough stress on anyone and find out
how quickly manners peel away
as lips pull back from teeth
just before an animal gets down to business.
All is stress in this place of becoming,
where friends beat friends unconscious
for the promise of a phone call home.
Families don't want to know that hearing from a son
has a price in blood: not now, and absolutely not
when the call comes from across the world.
They want to meet their boys at the airport, feel
our solid weight; they want to recognize us by shape alone
once we're made into survivors.

5.

Once we're made into survivors,
we're all of us unsteady: we know that
we'll make our old friends uncomfortable,
that our families will piss us off trying to cheer us up
because we won't understand how cheery
is enough for them. Our mothers can't read
our expressions any longer—if it's smiles they want,
they're going to have to get us drunk.
None of that matters because we're Supermen now,
and if we're to be invincible the price
is becoming strangers to everyone
but each other. We make the expected noises,
fool those who need to be fooled—
only we can see each other's faces.

6.

Only we can see each other's faces,
packed in like the teeth on a zipper—my leg,
his leg, my other leg, his other leg—
on the cargo-netting seats of a C-130,
but we're not looking into faces;
collapsed into each other like string-cut
marionettes, we're sleeping or pretending
that flying into combat bores us.
Supermen sleep in transit every time—
no guarantees of when we'll sleep again, or if,
so we tuck chin to flak jacket and light out
for anywhere else. We wake bitter and panicked,
plane dropping too sharply for Stinger missiles, look up,
read the taut, terrible smiles.

7.

Read the taut, terrible smiles
and return them; coming in for the landing
that finally puts boots to sand,
fists cramped from clenching,
tension bleeding gums and locking jaw
because they are shooting the fucking plane—
the sound like gravel road plinking an undercarriage—
so just smile and think payback,
think *that's all these bastards get for free.*
Though here payback costs you too,
billed to your home address—scaring civilians that cut in line,
or screaming out the car window in traffic,
from now on violence is your first option:
the threshold has been exceeded.

8.

The threshold has been exceeded
and it's a good thing—there's no other way
to face this antiseptic-and-desert stink,
the bomb-chewed bodies wheeling
past in a flash of gurney-chrome and shouting,
trailing rapid-fire drops of cast-off spatter
that you shouldn't be able to hear hit the deck.
But you can hear it all the same.
Blood is loud here, and there's so much
in a body, so much that can be lost
and still leave a person behind, deflated
but animate. My dog tag says B Positive—
a just-in-case that sounds madly like advice
from the letters we've been getting lately.

9.

From the letters we've been getting lately
we've learned more than we ever asked:
that Jones' wife bought a horse with his money,
and the Gunny's kid stole a car,
brothers, fathers, mothers, sisters have gotten married
and my uncle died of stroke,
that Reed hasn't heard from his girl for months,
but that story gets old quick out here.
Here's what we don't write back:
We're still getting mortared.
Yesterday Engles became the first of us
to kill someone—two someones—for sure. The best
things their letters carry are the smell, and their ignorance:
it sounds like our war is going well.

10.

It sounds like our war is going well—
the big guns boom a rebuttal
to the sharp blast of an incoming mortar,
keep reverse-triangulation's promise
that no one shoots at us twice. Artillery gunners,
killing with trigonometry, must be
the only people in this whole country who go to sleep satisfied,
missions truly accomplished.
New guys hate artillery until they learn
how to hear—the quick chatter
of our SAWs, harsh AK coughs,
incoming's treble, outgoing's bass—
you can hear the kind of day you'll have tomorrow,
though it doesn't matter to anyone else.

II.

Though it doesn't matter to anyone else,
for a time we'll live or die
based on how clearly we can see
through these iron sights.
Positive ID demands we process
this light streaming through our eyes—
hands might be hidden, robes might conceal
anything, but hostility looks the same on any face.
The trick, after, is no longer seeing,
making memory unvisible, putting it away.
Of course, sometimes we'll sleep,
though maybe less and less, fighting
sight we don't know is alive
until we bring it home.

12.

Until we bring it home,
we have no idea what we're carrying,
the terrible gravity of coming back,
everything becoming heavy faster
than the speed of pain. We can't bear
the adulation, the thanks for our *service*,
as if we knew what that word meant, before.
Replies fall leaden from our mouths.
Is it any wonder some of us can
no longer breathe the atmosphere?
Test pilots of drone strikes, remote detonations,
we're reflecting older faces—home life moves
at the speed of light and if we catch up
we find our lives have been cut short.

13.

We find our lives have been cut short—
people ask about the past like we're old men
already, like we've used up all the milestones
we're allotted in this life. They mean no harm,
our questioners, only want to know
what it was like without having to go,
the same way I wonder how it feels
to swim with sharks—which is to say, idly.
We tell the same stories over and over,
elongated moments described in two sentences,
poorly, without traumatizing our listeners,
beating familiar tracks in our minds,
and if those paths seem short, safe,
measure them instead in depth.

14.

Measure them instead in depth,
and you will understand these young old men
better. They haven't legally bought a beer,
and yet they've seen friends die,
known survivor's rage, teeth cracked from grinding,
the guilt, the desire to kill everyone
everywhere, leave this desert clean,
a reminder to the world—live better.
If they scare you, it is because they should;
the quiet ones, the loudly self-destructive,
the smiling, always seeming happy to be back,
though their eyes tell a different story
of time lived in breadth, not length—
measure them instead in depth.

15. HOW WE LIVE

It's damned difficult,
teeth gritted around the last syllable: *Marine,*
and it becomes easier to imagine killing—
horrors come naturally to us all, after a fashion.
Once we're made into survivors
only we can see each other's faces,
read the taut, terrible smiles:
the threshold has been exceeded.
From the letters we've been getting lately,
it sounds like our war is going well,
though it doesn't matter to anyone else
until we bring it home—
we find our lives have been cut short,
measure them instead in depth.

III

David Gomez: El Paso, Texas

We stood at ease, ate their food,
and told only the good stories,
while he lay in the parlor
wearing Blues we dressed him in.
I spoke for our platoon, although
I'd never seen Mexican grief—
the grim faces of his men,
the tearing of his mother's breast.
I told the truth as well I could:
you don't get the same son back.
A knife, sharpened for violent work,
is less knife than when it started.
He'd been broken some to get him right,
so he could do what we all did
and the life he'd kept for all of us
he'd taken from himself.
We carried him out when it was time
and we burnt him like Achilles,
saying how fitting and proper it was
to leave nothing behind.

Get Some

It terrifies me that I miss it.
In summer, I park my car in the sun,
return to heat like water
and I flash to steam, leather scalding my neck
as I'm immersed again:

Hudson's femoral, brachial—
did it matter what its name was
when it jetted hot, even in the heat,
driving the spray of his life
into our fear-faces, and the smell of it baked
into the radio, burning copper and meat,
never left the humvee, any humvee, after.

Screaming like laughter,
arming his blood and tears of joy
from my eyes, *you should have killed me,*
barrel stuck out the window, jolting
glass dust and hot brass into my lungs
and I feel great, shutter-clicking
a lifetime of dreams through the cordite smoke
while my mind flees, shows me
in detail better than it was
the last time I had sex, just in case.

I am lighter now, more than forty pounds—
flak jacket with ceramic inserts,
helmet, gas mask, bayonet, and M-16 and magazine,
magazine, magazine, magazine, magazine and magazine,
enough to kill fifteen dozen people—
or just three, sixty times over.
I don't know how to carry myself without
that weight, my steps too light,
like mist waiting to evaporate
when the sun finally burns me off.

Hadji

I thought I was ready for us to meet, Hadji,
as my convoy rumbled through your city.
I'd shot Expert, could keyhole
shots in the necks of man-shaped targets
at five-hundred yards—you'd be much closer.

I thought I knew how you'd go down, Hadji,
but targets don't bleed, or scream, or cling so
goddamn hard to life. 5.56's jump
on impact, go in the leg, out the neck
and covering the holes didn't keep you alive.

I thought I'd be all right, Hadji—
went home on my feet, though I can't
remember how to sleep
a night through. Yesterday a girl
hit my cart at the grocery store.
I hadn't thought of you in months, didn't then,
just stood staring at cheeses
like they mattered,
wanting so much
to unclench my fists and fly the fuck apart.

Conversation We Might Have, If We Could

I.

In my dream, your body
walks into my office hours,
makes itself at home
and I talk to it.

Even before the recoil I knew
I hit you, before the recoil I'm still doing,
the grit in my mouth, the wish
in my throat that I'd bent down
to close your eyes against the sand.

Don't mistake me: this is not an apology.
I'd do it again, every time.

You turned broadside to me,
running for the alley
you never reached,
and I couldn't have missed
you if I'd tried.

Not a beautiful thing to be good at, shooting,
but talent just wants to be used, even with nothing
to show for it except all the ways
you will never again move in this world.
Or me either.

II.

For some time I'd hidden from my students that I fought a war.

The day it came out, a student asked about you, indirectly. He didn't think over the question, just opened his mouth and let fly, "Did you ever kill anyone?"

I just stared at him, the others—sweet kids—growing apologetic on his behalf. I said his name, said I wasn't mad, but that he'd asked an inappropriate question.

My student apologized. I told him it was fine, but he spent a quiet class that day. He wanted to talk after. I didn't.

NATO Phonetic

Alpha Company went outside the wire
that night, got hit in the same place
as Bravo had the week before.
An EFP tore through a Humvee,
scattered pieces of Lutz, Garcia, and Charlie
all over the Euphrates delta—
we heard the echo inside the wire,
learning the foxtrot at the MWR tent
from a clean civilian woman
in a low-cut shirt and short golf skort. She jumped
at the blast and I laughed, told her
welcome to Hotel Fallujah, lady
and tried to dance better, imagining
my fingers in that hair, dark as India ink,
pretending I was only staring at the little gold
nameplate—*Juliette*—over her heart.

At chow, I heard EOD say
there was only about a kilo of explosive
behind the metal plate (disguised by the lid
on a barrel of lima beans from our very own
humanitarian aid package) set off
by the particular frequency of a Humvee engine
passing by a hidden mike.

The TV blared CNN headlines—
November deadliest month
of 2006. That was the day
Corporal Oscar came back from his two weeks of
leave, told us about his expatriate papa in Quebec—
didn't support the war—while oiling
his M-16, (*gonna sleep with it too, Romeo?*)
like he'd missed it.

Only Charlie survived, started a different
kind of war with Bethesda,
Walter Reed, Sierra Military Health Services
and Veterans Affairs before he could get a new fake leg.
Racists, he says, *don't care*
about a dark green Marine.

He gets around all right these days
though he won't be doing the tango anytime
soon. He irons the crease
where his uniform trouser pins up,
its razor line his only symbol of victory.

I promise I'll visit him,
take my white ass down to the South Bronx,
bring some whiskey and Xanax and root against
the Yankees in their own house.
He tells me *they'll tear you up, Lack,*
even with a Zulu Warrior
like me next to you.
Before I can think to stop myself
I say, *Fuck 'em, Charlie, I'm bulletproof.*

In Heaven There Are No Doors

"This heaven feels homeless and requires love more than ever now . . ."
   William Olsen

If I am dead, I reject this heaven,
the doors growing in numbers stretching
up and down before and behind me,
out of work in my combat loadout,
downcast eyes on downscale thresholds,
desert prizefighters on the other sides.
I'm reminded, as my squadmate pushes me
to breach (be empty, Lord, please)
that *threshold* means also *far as I can go*
and *much as I can stand* in these suspended instants
when murder changes hands and we exchange fire
with men no less strange than ourselves.
In this heaven hearts break
over furnace streets
that I try to wish out of existence.
I gather shriveled leaves in handfuls
and crush them into fragments.
Suspended inside my gear, I stumble
downhill in boiling boots, toward
the people with half-faces above their scarves,
hands hidden, like despair is winning in this city
of doors, of rooms to be cleared in quarters
so close the shots travel backward
through time, sweep men into history.
What is it about these people—they never, ever look up,
just keep trying to stare themselves into the graces of a kinder god.
It's so dry everyone weeps blood.
Wilson was killed by the roadside, frozen in flame,
Hudson was killed in a turret, sprung in three places,

Dean was killed by a collapsing pediment when this heaven
began raining stone.
Ordinary losses—when your number's up, you die
in a moment's exhilaration or choking to death on a lemon
and this heaven's unspooling faster than we can reel in
because in this heaven hope is a function of effort.

Heaven is not squat walls covered in broken glass
so utterly unhome, by which I mean
shadowing my retinas, a dark backdrop
blotting my day-to-day,
when life is the movie set and all's real behind my eyelids.
The aperture sticks open and the film bleaches and burns.
In a bar I like because no one speaks,
I sit in the corner, put the table in front of me
so everyone has to cross my sightline
on their way up and back—
some don't even look, just think *they don't even look* my way
and I could be anyone with a steel needle
and hummingbird's precision
lunging across the table.
I want to stress them until they snap.
The ultimate tensile strength of self, like wire
drawn thin too fast—it's called *necking*
when you start to give in the middle,
and there's no popping back
now that the only life is other than your own,
people who couldn't begin to understand talking down to you.

Self-Portrait in Public

Look how I measure
everyone who passes:
their open hands,
their open faces, unprotected
necks—myself, I hunch
my shoulders almost
all the time, lock
my jaw and tuck my chin
under the guise of looking
over my glasses.

I'm thinking: *this one's never*
been punched in the face
in his life; this guy
wrestled in high school;
I'd need a bat
to knock out a man
without a neck;
that one I'd have to hurt
permanently,
and quick.

Small Talk

Thank me for my service,
then—now that's out of the way—
feel free to be as rude as you like.
Call me 'soldier' though I am a Marine,
make no apology, just lay hands on me
with impunity, clap my shoulder and smile
as if at a secret only we two share, as if we
share anything at all.

Keep leaning forward, keep asking me
about the *action* I've seen as if you know
what you're talking about. You want
to know if I've killed anyone.
I'll tell you but you have to
come closer.

I'll tell you how recoil jolts,
how by the time you bring your sights
around again the target
is gone, one way or the other,
how bullets are designed to stay inside bodies
and so men facedown could almost be asleep,
how you always, always get blood on your hands—come here,

and I'll describe the half-moons of dull red
at the base of my fingernails,
their resistance to hot water, cold water,
degreaser, dish soap, sanitizer, confession,
contrition, every damn thing I ever learned
about getting clean.

You ask if I like video games
in 1080p, if I can comment on the accuracy
of the program that simulates blood splatter
but what you really want to know,

the inevitable design
of this whole night's wheedling
is if you could
kill anyone
and I know, of course
I know, I can tell a killer
now just by looking at him
and I'll tell you
but only in a whisper
so come closer,
where I can reach you.

First Supper Back

I understand that you've never relied, Mother,
on non-verbal signals of the hands, arms,
to make yourself understood in situations
where speaking leads to killing—

yourself more than likely among the dead
and rightly, for making all the noise: or maybe

you're simply inured to the repeated,
insistent, jabbing of my fork, that way, *that* way,
even (though this is a stretch, Ma)
the audible grinding of teeth,
cramped muscles I've knotted
in the battle, the epic struggle,
though I love you, to keep
from burying these tines in you

just once, just to break that lazy, civilian oblivion—
we learn best what we learn in pain,
and you must be taught to see me now.

A Reminder I Don't Need

I intended to move the bee
butting against my kitchen window,
to reward his tenacity—
he would break the window
or himself but never stop.
I liked that. A Marine Corps bee.
I wanted it to work,
the pacifist glass-and-paper

transport—redeploy this brother
bee to his natural environment.
I settled the cup
over him gently, like setting a trip-wire,
eyes wide, breath held,
careful not to set him off
as I eased the paper under him.

But I pulled the cup too firm,
too fast, trapped the bee hard
by a wall he could not see or understand
and ripped him in half.

A long, deep strobe of guilt—
That's who you are now.

Suicide Days

The cat litter needs changing,
the dinner I have not yet planned—
let alone cooked—nevertheless
must be eaten, all my goddamn clothes
are dirty again, and these meaningless
life-or-life decisions piling up like the dishes,
could be stopped if I wanted.

Today I could run
back to my recruiter, out to the desert
or the mountains, I don't give a fuck
just give me my weapon again
and something to point it at besides myself
because either way this trigger is pulling.

Without Regard

Right now I am picking up hair ties. Our cat scatters them nightly, regardless of where my wife leaves them, which is all over the house. They spatter the sink's ledge, make rings on our coffee table, constrict furniture arms. It is a game we all play. I get knee-bound, peer under the couch.

Now, in a hallway I will never be able to describe, I gulp crematorium-hot air and drip sweat onto the flak-jacketed back of my best friend, who will breach the door and survive the next several seconds. When I knee him he moves as if lives depend on it. Lives depend on it.

But now I am picking up hair ties. I have found a pirate-stash of them sheltered in the lee of the big bookcase. My focus sharpens like stretching cramped muscles, like aiming down the sight, and I fix their location in memory. I relish it, this obsolete talent I and others once lived by, and reach shoulder-deep. I do not grope.

Scanning

The double-yellow line bisects my car,
the left and right ditches as far from us as possible,
and I'm scanning: jumble of children's toys,
innocently small, two hubcaps in a tree,
a large, headless carcass but there aren't any
wires coming out of it, Coke can,
mysteriously upright, mangled soccer ball,
folding chair, battered road sign, window frame.
I'm dismissing the scraps of paper and plastic,
but that metal garbage can could be lethal
if filled with rocks or glass, or jacks dipped
in shit and why is it jutting over the line as if reaching—
the long black dirt track says it was dragged
into place just there for us—

My wheels churn up the opposite shoulder
and my wife looks up from her book and asks
What's the matter?
I take her hand, shake my head,
Nothing, love. Just something in our road.

Mission Statement

I'm going to sit down today
and write a poem that won't make my wife cry.
One that's not about war, or if it is,
about some uplifting facet
only a poet could notice—maybe
a desert rose that survived where
my platoon mates did not
or the boy we didn't kill
because he put away his cell phone.

I'm going to write a poem
as if I don't have nightmares about
a lost rifle, of a magazine
loaded with misfires, click-
click-clicking, of fists made of feathers
and a blunted bayonet.

That poem will not be
like this one. It will be
about some best version of me,
who works in an office and would never
threaten to kill someone for
cutting him off in traffic.

I'll read it to her, and we'll smile as if
she has not learned to tell by my breathing
when she should jostle me—as if she
hasn't had to learn the perfect technique:
gentle so as to not wake me,
but always enough to
get me out.

ABOUT THE AUTHOR

Bruce Lack is a graduate of the Helen Zell Writers' Program at the University of Michigan. He served honorably in the United States Marine Corps from 2003-2007, at Camp Pendleton, California, and Fallujah, Iraq. He lives in Portage, Michigan.

Selected by Robert A. Fink, Service is the twenty-fourth winner of the Walt McDonald First-Book Competition in Poetry. The competition is supported generously through donated subscriptions from *The American Scholar, the Atlantic Monthly, The Georgia Review, Gulf Coast, The Hudson Review, The Massachusetts Review, Poetry, Shenandoah,* and *The Southern Review.*